the *tapas* cookbook

the *tapas* cookbook

seventy delicious recipes

to capture the flavours of spain

Adrian Linssen with Sara Cleary

TED SMART

A QUINTET BOOK

This edition produced for
The Book People Ltd
Hall Wood Avenue
Haydock
St Helens WA11 9UL

ISBN 1-85613-746-5

This book was designed and produced by
Quintet Publishing Limited
6 Blundell Street, London, N7 9BH

CREATIVE DIRECTOR: richard dewing
ART DIRECTOR: lucy parissi
DESIGNERS: simon balley and joanna hill
PROJECT EDITOR: amanda dixon
EDITOR: gail dixon-smith
PHOTOGRAPHER: tim ferguson hill
FOOD STYLIST: alison austin

Picture Credits
Travel Ink: pages 7(b), 8(t)
Life File: pages 6(t), (b), 7(t), 8(b), 9(t)

Special thanks to Ana Henriquez Marteau for her help with the
subtleties of the Spanish language, and for supplying the recipes for
Garlic Potatoes and Russian Salad.

Typeset in Great Britain
by Central Southern Typesetters, Eastbourne
Manufactured in Singapore by
Pica Colour Separation Overseas Pte Ltd
Printed in Singapore by Star Standard Industries Pte Ltd
Material in this book previously appeared in *Tapas*
by Adrian Linssen with Sara Cleary

Some recipes in this book use raw eggs.
Because of the slight risk of salmonella, raw eggs should
not be served to the very young, the ill or
the elderly, or to pregnant women.

contents

above: **Hotel bar in Colmenar, Andalusia.**

Ripe with the flavours of history and seasoned with the tastes of modern time, Spanish *tapas* are mouthwatering little dishes of delight.

According to Spanish folklore, the first *tapa* was a slice of cured ham thrown hastily atop a glass of sherry to keep out the flies. The ham was so popular it gave birth to the tradition of Spanish *tapas*—literally "lids" or "covers". Today cured ham, *jamón serrano*, is served alongside dishes from all over Spain; from fresh squid and salted almonds to stewed olives and goat's cheese. They present an abundance of tastes, smells and colours; and invite the uninhibited mixing of each—truly both a gourmand's and a chef's delight!

Tapas bars are at the center of every Spanish community, from the remote, relaxed mountain villages to the busy, crowded city districts. Twice a day, like clockwork, Spaniards congregate at their favourite local bar for a chilled sherry or a glass of white wine, conversation with their friends and, of course, *tapas*.

below: **Orange stall in Javea, Alicante.**

A good *tapas* bar is an Aladdin's cave of indulgence, filled with gastronomic treasures. Arranged along the counter is an assortment of cheeses, prawns, scallops, garlic, chicken, omelettes and salads. From the ceiling hang cured hams and stacked against the back wall are dusty bottles of wine.

Served as *media ración*, or appetizers, flavourful dishes like Garlic Mushrooms, Fried Squid, or Goat's Cheese with Tarragon and Garlic Marinade awaken the palate while leaving room for heartier dishes. Make no mistake, however; *tapas* are not limited in size, ingredients or to a fixed course in a meal. They are equally delicious eaten as *ración*—with enough for a group to share as bar snacks, or for one hungry bar-goer to eat as a main course.

above: Fishermen in Nerja, Andalusia.

below: Menu of *raciones*, Madrid.

Eating "*tapas*-style" can spice up any occasion. Impress your guests at your next barbecue with some *tapas*-inspired dishes: throw on a few Marinated Lamb Cutlets and Spicy Moorish Kabobs, and serve with Garlic Potatoes and Tomato Salad with Olives.

Add a taste of the sea with Spicy Monkfish Brochettes or Bacon-wrapped Shrimp with Sour Cream. For special festivities get extra tangy with Oysters Bloody Mary—mix an ice-cold Bloody Mary, carefully open the oysters, loosen from the shell, pour in the juice... and swallow!

Even vegetarians can relish in their *tapas*. Many main and side dishes can be tastily prepared without meat: favorites include Roast Potatoes in Sweet Hot Sauce; Three Peppers in

above: **Tiled façade in Alicante province.**

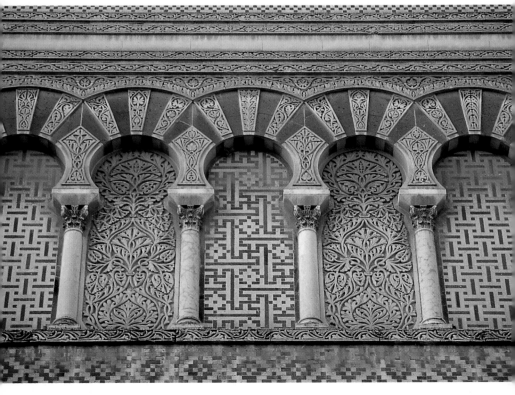

above: **Mosque exterior in Cordoba, Andalusia.**

Tomato and Garlic; Green Beans Tapa; and the national staple, the Spanish Omelette—or *Tortilla*.

The more exotic and more involved *tapas* are ideal served at special celebrations. Lobster and Chicken Brochettes, Chicken Livers with Sherry Vinegar and Spanish-style Squid or Chicken Pies—or *Empanadas*—make tantalisingly exotic main dishes. Slice open an *Empanada*, and the wafting aroma is guaranteed to bring smiles of anticipation to the faces of your guests. On a hot day, what better than a colourful chilled Prawn Salad—or *Ceviche*—to cool you down and spice things up?

Tapas can be served in a shell or on a brochette, with or without a sauce. They can be large or small, hot or cold, complex or simple. The dishes range from vegetable to egg and cheese, fish, shellfish

above: **Archway and cobbled street in Frigliana, Andalucia.**

and a host of fresh and cured meats. The recipes are adaptable and there is something for everyone and for every occasion. The only difficulty lies in the choosing.

Note: Use a vegetable oil of your choice in recipes where an unspecified oil is called for.

These recipes, unless otherwise indicated, make *tapa* for four. This is intended as a rough guide only as *tapas*, by their very nature, vary in size.

Marisco

Seafood Tapas

Scallops with Lime and Crab

Vieiras con Cangrejo y Lima

12 small to medium, or 6
large scallops (slice the
latter across
horizontally)
Juice of 4 limes
Juice of 2 oranges
1½ Tbsp brandy
1 small piece of root ginger,
finely chopped
Salt and freshly ground
black pepper
White crab meat, to garnish

preparation

To prise open the scallops place them dark side of
shell down and slip a sharp knife through the hinge to
sever the muscle which holds the scallop to the shell.

Trim away the muscular "foot". Wash and place in the
refrigerator, in the cleaned shells, on a tray.

Mix the lime juice, orange juice, brandy, ginger and
seasoning together and spoon over the scallops.
Marinate for 4 to 6 hours. The scallops will go
opaque and be firm to the touch when ready.

Lightly season the crab meat and flake over
the scallops.

Serve well chilled.

Scallops in Tomato Sauce

Vieiras en Salsa Tomate

12 small or 6 large scallops
55 g/2 oz butter
155 ml/5 fl oz dry white wine
100 g/4 oz grated Parmesan cheese
Lemon wedges, to serve

For the sauce
3 Tbsp butter
1 heaped Tbsp flour
570 ml/1 pt milk, warmed
½ Tbsp tomato purée
1 tsp garlic, crushed
1 tsp sugar
2 large tomatoes, peeled and finely chopped
1 Tbsp double cream
55 g/2 oz grated Parmesan cheese
½ tsp freshly ground black pepper

For the potato
900 g/2 lb potatoes
Salt
85 g/3 oz butter
2 egg yolks
2 Tbsp single cream, warmed
Salt and freshly ground black pepper
2 tsp parsley, chopped

to prepare the scallops

Open by placing in the oven at 450°F/230°C/Gas Mark 8 for a few minutes. Cut out the scallop with a sharp knife, trim off the "foot" and wash well. Wash the shells and keep to one side.

Separate the pink coral from the white of the scallop and keep both in the refrigerator.

to prepare the sauce

Melt the butter, stir in the flour and cook to a sandy texture. Gradually whisk in the warmed milk, then the tomato purée, garlic and sugar. Stir occasionally and simmer for 20 minutes to cook the flour. Lower the heat and stir in the chopped tomatoes, cream, cheese and pepper. Keep to one side until needed.

While the sauce is cooking, prepare the mashed potato. Peel, wash and chop the potatoes into even pieces, place in salted water, bring to the boil and cook until soft. Drain thoroughly, return to the pot, cover and place over a low heat, shaking occasionally to dry them out. Mash with 2 tablespoons butter. With a wooden spoon, mix in the yolks and the rest of the butter. Beat in the warm cream and season well. Stir in the chopped parsley. Take a piping bag, with a star nozzle, and fill it with the potato.

to cook the scallops

Melt the butter and when hot, add the scallops (keeping back the pink corals, as they take less cooking) and turn to seal both sides. Add the wine, bring to the boil, then add the pink corals and simmer for 3 minutes.

Place the shells on a baking tray and spoon 1 teaspoon of sauce into each shell. Place a scallop and a coral back into each shell. Spoon the sauce over. Pipe the potato in little stars around the edge of the shell. Sprinkle the cheese over and place in a hot oven (425°F/220°C/Gas Mark 7) for 5 minutes or until cheese is browned. Serve with lemon wedges.

Fried Squid

Sepia Frita

900 g/2 lb squid, cleaned
3 eggs, beaten
Flour
Salt and freshly ground
black pepper
Lemon wedges, to serve

to clean the squid

Cut off the legs just below the eyes and keep to one side. Squeeze the top of the legs and the beak will pop out; discard it. Empty the body sac over the sink, by thrusting the fingers under the plastic-like backbone. Pull out the backbone and discard it. Pull the innards carefully, so that they come out in one piece, and discard. Rinse the inside of the sac. Remove the fins firmly from where they join the body. The purple membraneous skin will then easily peel off. Rinse well and slice the body across into 13 mm/¹/₂-inch thick rings. Combine with the legs and rinse again. Place a pot of water on the stove, with enough water to cover the squid. When boiling, add the squid and blanch for 1 minute. Remove and cool immediately under cold water. The squid are now ready for further use.

preparation

Mix the eggs well over the squid, using your hands. Season. Slowly add enough flour, mixing thoroughly to a thick paste. Heat the deep-fryer to 365°F/165°C and carefully lower the squid piece by piece, and in batches, into the oil. Shake and fry to a golden colour. Remove, drain, season, and serve with lemon wedges.

Marinated Whitebait

Chanquetes Fritos

450 g/1 lb bag frozen
whitebait, defrosted (for
about 2 hours at room
temperature)
1 Tbsp parsley, chopped
2 tsp garlic, crushed
Juice of 2 lemons (or enough
to cover the fish while
they marinate)
2 shallots, finely chopped
2 tsp freshly ground
black pepper
½ tsp salt
4 Tbsp olive oil

preparation

Remove heads of fish. Split lengthwise for the larger
ones, and leave the small ones whole. Pull out the
bone of the larger ones.

Place on a tray or in a square dish (not a metal dish).
Cover with the parsley, garlic, lemon juice, shallots
and seasoning.

Leave to marinate for 24 hours in the refrigerator.

Drain off the excess juice. Cover with the oil, leave for
one hour, and serve.

Deep-fried Whitebait

Chanquetes en Escabeche

450 g/1 lb frozen whitebait
115 ml/4 fl oz milk, at room
temperature
Flour, to coat
Oil, to fry
Salt, preferably sea salt
Lemon wedges, to serve

preparation

Shake the frozen whitebait into the milk. If the milk is
too cold, small ice particles will form; if this happens,
add a few drops of hot water.

Shake the fish thoroughly into the flour. Toss
thoroughly in a sieve to remove excess flour.

Place the fish in a deep fryer and fry in hot oil for
3 minutes in 2 or 3 batches; too many together will
stick in the basket. If you do not have a frying basket,
pan-fry in 2 tablespoons of oil until cooked through.

Sprinkle with the salt and serve immediately with
lemon wedges.

Fried Sardines

Sardinas Fritas

12 sardines
1½ Tbsp seasoned flour
Salt and freshly ground
black pepper
Oil, to fry
Lemon wedges, to serve

**For the marinade, blend
together:**
2 tsp parsley, chopped
4 Tbsp lemon juice
½ tsp garlic, crushed
Salt and freshly ground
black pepper
4 Tbsp olive oil

Ingredients for the sauce/dip
1 large tomato, skinned and
chopped
1 small green pepper, seeded
and chopped
½ small onion, chopped
Enough mayonnaise to bind
Salt and freshly ground
black pepper

to prepare the sardines

Take the sardines (if the head is on, leave it) and cut through the abdomen lengthwise without cutting through the bone. Butterfly the fish.

Paint the marinade on the fish, and leave to marinate for 20 minutes.

Shake the flour over the fish, dusting until well covered. Shake off any excess flour. Season.

Heat the oil until hot and fry the sardines turning to brown both sides.

to prepare the sauce/dip

Mix all the ingredients together, then either spoon onto plates with the sardines or use as a dip.

Serve with lemon wedges.

Monkfish with Anchovy Sauce

R a p e   c o n   S a l s a   d e   A n c h o a s

450 g/1 lb monkfish, skinned, cleaned, and cubed
1 Tbsp freshly ground black pepper
Flour
115 ml/4 fl oz olive oil
4 Tbsp anchovy paste
Parsley, to garnish

preparation

Season the fish and lightly dust with flour.

Heat the oil in a pan, add fish pieces and lower heat. Cover and cook for 4 to 6 minutes, until the flesh is still quite springy and very slightly underdone. Remove from the oil and keep warm.

Add the anchovy paste to the pan and bring to the boil.

Taste for a strong, sharp, peppery flavour.

Return the fish to the pan, stir and serve garnished with parsley.

Spicy Monkfish Brochettes

Culiacin de Rape

900 g/2 lb monkfish tail
235 ml/8 fl oz water
5½ Tbsp lime juice

For the sauce
4 red chillies, seeded and chopped
Olive oil
2 large tomatoes, peeled and chopped
1 tsp dried oregano
1 tsp freshly ground black pepper
1 tsp cumin seed
1 tsp ground ginger
2 tsp garlic
565 ml/1 pt fish stock
½ large cucumber
1 medium red onion
Lime wedges, to serve
Tabasco sauce, to taste

preparation

For this recipe, you will need six large skewers.

Skin, bone and cube the fish. Marinate in the water and lime juice for four hours, or overnight if possible.

Fry the chillies in a little olive oil, until dark. Add the chopped tomato, oregano, black pepper, cumin seed, ginger, garlic and fish stock to the chillies. Bring to the boil and simmer for 10 minutes. Remove from the heat.

Cut the cucumber into 6 mm/¼-inch rounds. Cut the red onion into eighths, by halving like an orange, then quartering each half.

Make up the skewers, by piercing a piece of onion, a piece of fish, a piece of cucumber, and so on, until the skewer is full. Coat liberally with the sauce. Serve with lime wedges and tabasco sauce.

Crab and Brandy Tartlets

Tartas de Cangrejo al Brandy

225 g/½ lb pastry
(see page 24 and halve
the quantity)
55 g/2 oz butter
½ medium onion, finely
chopped (preferably a
red onion, as the flavour
is milder)
1 tsp tomato purée
Pinch of sugar
155 ml/5 fl oz white wine
450 g/1 lb crab meat
Pinch of nutmeg
1 Tbsp parsley, chopped
Salt and freshly ground
black pepper
Juice of 2 oranges
2 Tbsp brandy
4 medium eggs and
1 extra yolk
285 ml/10 fl oz milk (or, for
a richer flavour, use the
same amount of single
cream)
75 g/2 oz grated manchego
cheese

preparation

This recipe makes 6 tartlets or one 20 cm/8 inch flan.

Prepare the pastry, rest it and line the moulds thinly. Bake blind: cover the pastry with foil, fill the case with dried beans and cook in a hot oven (450°F/230°C/Gas Mark 8) for 5 to 8 minutes.

to prepare the filling

In a pan, melt the butter. Add the onion and cover. Cook gently until the onion is soft.

Add the tomato purée, sugar, then white wine. Stir in the crab meat, nutmeg, parsley, salt and pepper. Add the orange juice and brandy, and simmer gently for 5 minutes. Stir and remove from heat. Allow to cool.

In a large bowl, blend the eggs with the milk or cream, whisking well.

Mix the crab mixture and manchego into the milk mix, check the seasoning and add some freshly ground black pepper.

Spoon the crab mixture into the pastry cases or flan base. Bake in a moderate oven (375°F/190°C/Gas Mark 5) until golden-brown and set, approximately 15 to 20 minutes.

Note: Manchego cheese is named after the Manchego sheep that grazed the plains of La Mancha, from whose milk it was originally made. It is Spain's most famous cheese. It is semi-firm, golden in colour, mellow-flavoured and melts beautifully when cooked. It is available in some supermarkets and most specialist cheese shops.

Lobster and Chicken Brochettes

Brochetas de Langosta y Pollo

2 fresh lobsters, each
680 g/1½ lb
2 chicken breasts, each
225 g/8 oz, cubed into
bite-size pieces
115 ml/4 fl oz dry white wine
115 ml/4 fl oz garlic and
tomato mayonnaise

**Garlic and tomato
mayonnaise**
To 285 ml/½ pt mayonnaise
add half its volume
tinned plum tomatoes
and mix in a food
processor, adding salt,
pepper and plenty of
garlic – 2 tsp for every
285 ml/½ pt mayonnaise
Lime wedges, to serve

preparation

You will need 6 skewers for this recipe.

Place the lobsters in a pot of boiling salted water. Lower heat and simmer for 5 minutes, or until they go pink. Remove from pot and allow to cool before handling.

Pull the tail section away from the head with a little twist. Remove the shells and cut the flesh into bite-size chunks.

Poach the chicken pieces in the white wine for 6 to 8 minutes. Cool.

Arrange the lobster and chicken alternately on the skewers.

Serve with the garlic and tomato mayonnaise and lime wedges.

Monkfish and Bacon Brochettes

Brochetas de Rape con Bacon

24 small button mushrooms
9 rashers lean bacon, sliced
in 7.5 cm/3 in lengths
450 g/1 lb monkfish tail,
boned, skinned and
cubed into small chunks
Olive oil
Salt and freshly ground
black pepper
8 Tbsp garlic and tomato
mayonnaise (see Lobster
and Chicken Brochettes,
page 19)

preparation

You will need 6 long skewers or 12 smaller sticks for this recipe.

Start by threading a mushroom on the skewer, then add a piece of folded bacon, then a piece of fish. Repeat until the stick is full and all the ingredients (or sticks) are used up.

Brush with olive oil and season. At this stage you may keep in the refrigerator until needed.

Cook by placing on an oiled baking sheet in a hot oven (425°F/220°C/Gas Mark 7) for approximately 7 to 8 minutes, until cooked through.

Dredge with garlic and tomato mayonnaise, and serve.

Smoked Fish Mayonnaise and Garlic Toast

Tostadas con Ajo Cubiertas de Pescado Ahumado

2 green peppers
4 Tbsp olive oil
Freshly ground black pepper
1 tomato, peeled and chopped
225 g/½ lb smoked mackerel
225 g/½ lb smoked cod (you could use cooked salted cod, but if you do, eliminate salt from the seasoning)
8 Tbsp garlic mayonnaise
6 slices of bread or 1 French stick
1 tsp garlic, crushed
2 Tbsp olive oil

Garlic mayonnaise
Add 2 tsp crushed garlic to 340 ml/12 fl oz mayonnaise and mix in food processor

preparation

Seed the peppers and cut into thin strips. Heat the oil in a pan and sauté the peppers over a low heat. Add black pepper and the tomato. Cover and sauté for 20 minutes, or until soft. Allow to cool.

Skin and bone the fish, mix the garlic mayonnaise into it and blend in a food processor with black pepper. It should reach double cream consistency; add more garlic mayonnaise if necessary.

Cut the bread into triangles or rounds and toast lightly. Brush on both sides with the garlic and 2 tablespoons olive oil. Bake in a hot oven (425°F/220°C/Gas Mark 7), until golden, approximately 3 to 5 minutes.

Spoon a little of the pepper mixture over each of the bread toasties. Spoon some smoked fish mix onto the pepper and serve—Spanish club sandwich style!

Fish Croquettes

Croquetas de Pescado

340 g/12 oz white fish
Enough milk to half-cover
the fish (approximately
235 ml/8 fl oz)
340 g/³⁄₄ lb mashed potatoes
4 Tbsp onion, chopped
Butter, to fry
¹⁄₂ tsp garlic, crushed
¹⁄₂ tsp paprika
1 Tbsp parsley, chopped
1 egg
1 heaped Tbsp flour
Egg wash (2 eggs beaten
with a little milk)
White breadcrumbs
Oil or butter, to fry
Lemon wedges, and garlic
and tomato mayonnaise
(see Lobster and Chicken
Brochettes, page 19),
to serve

preparation

Wash the fish, half-cover with milk and poach in the oven for 15 minutes. Remove all skin, then bone and flake the fish. Set aside.

Prepare the mashed potatoes (both the fish and the potatoes can be prepared in advance).

Soften the onion in a little butter, add the garlic, paprika and parsley. Stir, and remove from the heat.

Mix the fish, potatoes and onion together, blending well, and season. Beat in the egg. The resulting mixture should be firm and pliable. Form the mix into little balls. Cover with flour, shake off any excess and pass through the egg wash to cover completely. Pass through the breadcrumbs, reshaping if necessary.

These may be deep-fried in hot oil (365°F/185°C) for 3 to 5 minutes until golden, or shallow-fried in melted butter, shaking the pan to brown evenly.

Serve with tomato and garlic mayonnaise and plenty of lemon wedges.

Spinach and Mussel Pot

Mejillones con Espinacas

450 g/1 lb spinach
1 medium onion, chopped
55 g/2 oz butter
1 tsp garlic, crushed
Pinch of nutmeg
Salt and freshly ground
black pepper
155 ml/5 fl oz dry
white wine
850 ml/1½ pts chicken stock
900 g/2 lb mussels, cleaned
(see tip below)
2 Tbsp single cream

preparation

Discard any stalks and large veins if using fresh
spinach, and wash thoroughly. **Note:** it is only
necessary to cook *fresh* spinach. Place in boiling
salted water for 2 minutes. Remove and cool under
cold water. Squeeze to remove moisture. Chop finely.

Fry the onion in the butter. Add the spinach, garlic,
nutmeg, salt and black pepper. Stir. Add the white
wine and turn up the heat. Cook for 5 minutes, until
the wine is almost dry. Add the stock and bring to the
boil. Stir and cook for 5 minutes. The consistency
should be that of double cream; if it's too thin,
continue cooking over heat, stirring until it thickens.

Add the mussels and cover the pot. Cook until the
mussels have opened, continuously shaking the pot.
Remove from the heat and season to taste. Pour into
bowls, evenly distributing the mussels. Swirl a little
cream over each, and serve.

tip

To clean fresh mussels, scrub clean under cold running
water and cut or pull off the long beard. Place in a
bowl of cold water and leave to stand for 2 to 3 hours.
This will allow the mussels to purge themselves of
sand. Discard any that float or are open.

Spanish Squid Pie

Empanada de Calamar

For the filling
4 Tbsp olive oil
1 medium onion, chopped
1 tsp garlic, crushed
*2 green peppers, seeded
and cut into fine strips*
*3 tomatoes, peeled and
halved*
*2 red chillies, seeded and
chopped*
*450 g/1 lb squid, cleaned as
in recipe for Fried Squid
(see page 13)*
235 ml/8 fl oz fish stock
235 ml/8 fl oz red Rioja wine
1 to 2 tsp salt
2 tsp paprika
Sprig of fresh thyme
*450 g/1 lb mussels, cleaned
(see tip, page 23) and
simmered in a little
boiling salted water for
5 minutes*
175 g/6 oz prawns
*Salt and freshly ground
black pepper*

**For the pastry
(makes approximately
450 g/1 lb dough)**
340 g/12 oz plain flour
*Generous 25 g/1 oz fresh
yeast (or ½ oz dried yeast)*
235 ml/8 fl oz milk, lukewarm
55 g/2 oz butter
2 eggs

*2 tomatoes, sliced and
peeled*
1 tsp salt
*1 egg yolk mixed with a
little milk, to glaze the pie*

to prepare the filling

Heat the oil in a large frying pan and gently cook the
onion and garlic. Add the peppers, tomatoes and
chillies, stir and cook for 10 minutes.

Add the rings of squid, with the chopped legs. Pour in
the stock and red wine, cover and cook for 20 minutes
over a moderate heat. Add the salt, paprika and thyme;
stir. If the mixture looks a little dry, add some water.
Remove mussels from the shells and add to the
mixture along with prawns. Remove from heat. Season.

to prepare the pastry

Sieve the flour into a bowl and make a well in the
centre. Crumble or sprinkle the yeast into the well. Pour
in the lukewarm milk and stir to dissolve the yeast.
Cover with a fine layer of flour. Do not blend this in.
Cover the bowl with a cloth and leave the mixture in a
warm place to rise until cracks in the covering layer of
flour appear, approximately 15 minutes.

While mixture is rising, melt butter in a pan and beat
in eggs. Stir in the salt and cool slightly.

Pour this egg and butter mixture over the floured
yeast in the bowl. Stir with a wooden spoon and beat
until the dough is thoroughly mixed.

Knead the dough, stretching and pulling with your
hands until it is dry and smooth. If it is too soft, add a
little more flour. Shape into a ball, place in the bowl
and dust lightly with flour. Cover with a tea towel.
Leave to rise in a warm place for 20 minutes. Knead
through again and leave to rise for a further 20
minutes, covered. It is now ready for use.

Grease and line a paella dish (dish for 2) with half the
dough. Add the filling; the pie will rise to fill dish.
Cover with slices of tomato and a little salt.

Roll out the remaining dough, sealing the edges well.
Glaze with the egg yolk and decorate as desired.
Leave to stand for 10 minutes before baking.

Bake in the oven at 400°F/200°C/Gas Mark 6 for
30 minutes. Leave to cool, and slice to serve.

Russian Salad

Ensaladilla Rusa

8 medium potatoes
1 medium carrot, diced
175 g/6 oz fresh peas
2 hard-boiled eggs, cooled,
peeled and cubed
One 200 g/7 oz tin tuna in
unsalted water, drained
and flaked
1 red pepper, diced
115 g/4 oz corn
40 g/1½ oz black olives
340 ml/12 fl oz mayonnaise

preparation

Put the potatoes in a large saucepan of water and
bring to the boil. Cover, lower the heat and simmer for
about 20 to 25 minutes, or until the potatoes are done.
Drain, and when cool, cut into 6 mm/¼ inch cubes.

Boil the carrot and peas for 3 to 5 minutes, until
lightly cooked. Drain.

Mix the potato with the egg, tuna, carrot, peas,
pepper, corn and olives in a large salad bowl.

Just before serving, add the mayonnaise to the salad
and toss to coat.

Mussels and Beans with Tomato

Mejillones con Judías en Salsa de Tomate

900 g/2 lb haricot beans
2 Tbsp olive oil
1 medium onion, chopped
2 rashers lean bacon, chopped
2 tsp garlic, crushed
1.1 l/2 pts chicken stock
900 g/2 lb mussels, cleaned (see *tip, page 23*)
1 large tomato, peeled and chopped
1 Tbsp parsley, chopped
Juice of 1 lemon
Salt and freshly ground black pepper

preparation

Soak the beans overnight in cold water, or use tinned beans if you prefer.

Heat the oil and fry the onion in it until soft. Add the bacon and stir. Add the beans and garlic, cover with the chicken stock and cook (20 minutes for tinned beans, 2 hours for dried, soaked beans).

Add the mussels, shake, cover and cook until the mussels open. Stir in the tomato, parsley and lemon juice. Season and serve in small bowls.

Anchovy and Mussels in White Wine Sauce

Mejillones con Anchoas San Sebastián

2 medium onions, chopped
2 green peppers, seeded
and finely chopped
8 Tbsp olive oil
1 tsp garlic, crushed
1 Tbsp paprika
450 g/1 lb fresh anchovies,
or 450 g/1 lb frozen
whitebait, defrosted
235 ml/8 fl oz dry white wine
235 ml/8 fl oz white wine
vinegar
285 ml/½ pt fish stock
900 g/2 lb mussels, cleaned
(see tip, page 23)

preparation

Fry the onions and peppers in the olive oil. Add the garlic and paprika, stir and add the fish. Simmer for approximately 5 minutes.

Pour on the wine, vinegar and stock, and bring to the boil. Add the mussels. Cover and cook, until the mussels open.

Season and serve in shallow dishes.

Fried Stuffed Mussels

Mejillones Fritos

1 medium onion, chopped

55 g/2 oz butter

290 ml/10 fl oz dry white wine

2 parsley stalks

A shaving of lemon peel

36 mussels (about 900 g/ 2 lb), cleaned (see tip, page 23)

140 g/5 oz cured ham (Spanish jamón serrano or Italian prosciutto)

55 g/2 oz soft white breadcrumbs

225 g/8 oz grated Parmesan cheese

Salt and freshly ground black pepper

2 Tbsp parsley, chopped

For the béchamel sauce

85 g/3 oz butter

100 g/3½ oz flour

285 ml/½ pt milk

Salt and freshly ground black pepper

preparation

Fry the onion in the butter in a saucepan. Add the wine, parsley stalks and lemon peel, and bring to the boil. Add the mussels, cover, and shake pan over high heat until the shells open. Remove the mussels with a slotted spoon and place in a bowl to cool. Strain the cooking liquid and keep it to add to the béchamel.

Remove the mussels from the shells (keeping the shells to one side). Mash the mussels with the ham or, if you prefer, wrap the mussels in small squares of ham. With a teaspoon put back into the shells, leaving space for the sauce.

to prepare the béchamel sauce

Melt the butter; stir in the flour. Warm the milk and add gradually, beating with a wooden spoon. Add the mussel liquid and simmer for 20 minutes. Season. The sauce should be quite thick. Spread the béchamel over the mussels and ham in the shells with a spoon or small palette knife. It will seal the mixture.

Mix the breadcrumbs with the cheese, and season. Sprinkle over the shells, place under a hot grill and cook until the cheese melts. Serve immediately, garnished with parsley.

Mussel, Prawn and Squid Tapa

Ensalada de Marisco

680 ml/1¼ pts fish stock
450 ml/16 fl oz white wine
450 g/1 lb unpeeled prawns
900 g/2 lb mussels, cleaned
(see p.23)
2 Tbsp olive oil
3 tsp garlic, crushed
3 tsp paprika
450 g/1 lb squid, cleaned
and blanched (see p.13)
8 Tbsp lemon juice
Salt and freshly ground
black pepper
Parsley, to garnish

preparation

In a saucepan, bring the stock and wine to the boil. Add the prawns and cook for 2 minutes. Remove from the pan with a slotted spoon, and drain.

Add the mussels to the stock, cover and cook until the shells open. Remove from the pan with a slotted spoon, and drain.

Heat the oil in another pan and add the garlic and paprika. Cook for 2 minutes, stirring continuously. Add the prawns, mussels, squid and lemon juice to the pan, season well and stir to mix all the ingredients. Heat through for 2 minutes and serve immediately, garnished with parsley.

King Prawns in Garlic

Langostinos al Ajillo

3 Tbsp olive oil
12 king prawns, fresh if
available; if not, cook
from frozen
2 tsp garlic, crushed
2 tsp paprika
2 Tbsp medium sherry
Lemon wedges, to serve

preparation

Heat the oil in a saucepan. For frozen prawns, lower heat, add the prawns to the oil, cover and cook for 6 minutes, until soft and heated through. For fresh prawns, add to the oil and cook until sizzling.

Add the rest of the ingredients and bring to the boil. Taste for seasoning and serve with lemon wedges.

Prawn Salad

Ceviche de Gambas

900 g/2 lb prawns or 450 g/
1 lb prawns and 450 g/
1 lb white fish
1.1 l/2 pts water
565 ml/1 pt lime juice
2 medium red onions, finely
chopped
2 Tbsp soy sauce
Salt and freshly ground
black pepper
2 cucumbers, seeded
and cubed
1 red pepper, seeded and cubed
1 bunch of dill, chopped
Tabasco sauce, to taste
Lime wedges, to serve

preparation

Shell prawns and skin and clean fish if using. Place in a large bowl.

Mix the ingredients for the marinade together (water, lime juice, red onions, soy sauce, salt and pepper) and pour over the prawns. Marinate for 20 minutes.

Add the cucumber, pepper slices and dill. Toss together in the bowl.

Spoon onto plates or into small bowls. Sprinkle with pepper and tabasco sauce. Serve with lime wedges.

Glazed King Prawns

Langostinos Glaseados

12 king prawns; if frozen,
defrost
2 egg yolks
285 ml/½ pt mayonnaise
1 Tbsp double cream
Freshly ground black pepper
½ tsp paprika
1 tomato, skinned and
chopped into small
squares
3 tsp garlic, crushed
Oil, to brush baking sheet
1 Tbsp parsley, chopped
Lemon or lime wedges and
garlic bread (see Garlic
Bread, page 40), to serve

preparation

Carefully remove the shell from the tails of the
prawns, keeping the heads intact.

Whisk the yolks into the mayonnaise with the cream,
black pepper, paprika, tomato and garlic.

Heat the grill and brush a baking sheet with oil.

Place the prawns on the baking sheet and spoon the
mayonnaise mixture over the tails.

Heat under the grill until brown spots appear.

Sprinkle the prawns with the chopped parsley and
serve immediately with lemon or lime wedges and
garlic bread.

King Prawns with Egg and Anchovy

Langostinos con Huevo y Anchoas

6 ready-cooked king prawns,
peeled (it is optional to
remove the heads)
3 hard-boiled eggs, shelled
and halved
6 anchovy fillets
6 black olives
170 ml/6 fl oz mayonnaise

preparation

You will need 6 cocktail sticks for this recipe.

On each stick, spear 1 prawn, half a cooked egg, a
rolled anchovy fillet and a black olive. Either cover in
mayonnaise or serve as a dip.

Bacon-wrapped King Prawns

Langostinos Envueltos en Tocineta

12 king prawns, peeled, leaving on the head and tail tip (defrost overnight if using frozen)
55 g/2 oz grated fresh mozzarella cheese
1 tsp freshly ground black pepper
12 rashers lean bacon, trimmed of the rind and excess fat
A little olive oil

preparation

Make a slit lengthwise along the back of the prawns, but do not cut through. Fill the slit with the cheese, mixed with the black pepper.

Wrap each prawn in one strip of bacon; start at the head, which should peep out, and slightly spiral the bacon to the tail. Secure with small wooden skewers if necessary. Brush with olive oil, and either grill or bake in a hot oven (450°F/230°C/Gas Mark 8) for 7 to 10 minutes. Meanwhile, prepare the dip.

For the sauce/dip
Soured cream
½ tsp each salt and freshly ground black pepper
Juice of ½ lemon

to prepare the sauce/dip

Mix all the ingredients together for the sauce, and serve with the hot prawns.

Oysters with Lime and Tabasco

Ostras Picantes con Lima

12 large fresh oysters
Tabasco sauce
Juice of 4 limes
Freshly ground black pepper
Lime wedges, to serve

preparation

Ask your fishmonger to shuck (open) your oysters for you. If this is not possible, follow the preparation instructions below.

Brush oysters under cold running water to clean. Place each oyster on a heavy chopping board, with the flat side up, and hit gently with a hammer to break off the thin edge of the shell.

Slide an oyster knife into the back of the shell and sever the hinge close to the flat upper shell. Remove upper shell and discard.

Cut the oyster from the lower shell and pick out any pieces of shell or grit. Place cleaned oyster in deep lower shell. Add 2 drops of tabasco sauce to each one. Sprinkle with lime juice and black pepper to serve.

Oysters Bloody Mary

Ostras Bloody Mary

340 ml/12 fl oz tomato juice
3 Tbsp vodka
5 drops Tabasco sauce
1 tsp Worcestershire sauce
1 Tbsp lemon juice
Salt and freshly ground
black pepper
12 fresh oysters
Cucumber, cut into cubes
Celery stalks (small, young
ones), cut into cubes
Lemon wedges, to serve

preparation

Mix a Bloody Mary using the tomato juice, vodka, Tabasco sauce, Worcestershire sauce, lemon juice, salt and pepper; mix in a blender with some ice cubes so that it is well chilled.

Open the oysters carefully (see page 34), and fill the shells with the Bloody Mary mix.

Sprinkle the cubed cucumber and celery over the shells, and serve with lemon wedges.

Tapas de Verdura

Vegetable Tapas

Asparagus and Lettuce Tarts

Tartas de Esparragos con Lechuga

450 g/1 lb asparagus, fresh,
or 450 g/1 lb tin of
asparagus spears
Juice of 1 lemon
1 medium onion, finely
chopped
55 g/2 oz butter
½ medium lettuce
1 clove garlic, crushed
Salt and freshly ground
black pepper
2 Tbsp dry white wine
225 g/½ lb pastry (see
page 24 and halve the
quantity)
285 ml/½ pt single cream
4 eggs and 1 extra egg yolk
55 g/2 oz grated cheese,
preferably manchego
(see note page 18)

One 20 cm/8 in flan tin, or
10 tartlet tins

preparation

If using fresh asparagus, discard the stringy white root part and chop the rest into 12 mm/½ inch pieces. Keep the tips separate.

Place the chopped asparagus in a pot of boiling salted water with the lemon juice added; keep back the tips. Simmer 8 to 10 minutes until just soft, adding the tips after 5 minutes. Remove from the heat, place a strainer over the pot and run cold water through it over the sink. The strainer will save the asparagus tips from breaking up into small pieces.

If using tinned asparagus, drain well and check that it is evenly chopped.

Gently cook the onion in the butter, covered, until soft. Add the finely chopped lettuce to the onion and stir. Add the garlic and seasoning. Pour in the white wine, stir and cook until the lettuce softens. If you need more liquid, add a little water. Cover and simmer for 5 minutes. Remove from the heat and allow to cool before mixing the asparagus with the onion and lettuce.

Grease and flour tartlet tins, or flan tin and position the pastry. Bake blind: cover the pastry with foil, fill the case with baking beans or rice and cook in a hot oven (450°F/230°C/Gas Mark 8) for 5 to 8 minutes. Remove the foil and beans.

Mix the cream with the eggs, and some salt and black pepper. Whisk well to break the egg white. Whisk in the grated cheese. Stir the lettuce and asparagus mix into the cream and egg mix, thoroughly blending the two so that the mix coats the vegetables. Spoon into the pastry tins, placing the tips on top.

Cook in a moderate oven (350°F/180°C/Gas Mark 4) for 10 minutes for tartlets or 15 minutes for flan-size.

The filling should be just firm to the touch and golden-brown when ready.

Aubergine with Cheese and Prawns

Berenjenas Rellenas de Gambas y Queso

1 large aubergine
Salt
75 g/2½ oz flour
Olive oil
285 ml/½ pt thick cheese
sauce (see below)
Parsley, to garnish

For the cheese sauce
55 g/2 oz butter
1 heaped Tbsp flour
285 ml/½ pt milk, warmed
½ small onion, chopped
1 bay leaf
Pinch of nutmeg
75 g/2½ oz grated manchego
or Parmesan cheese
1 Tbsp single cream
1 egg yolk
175 g/6 oz prawns
Salt and freshly ground
black pepper

preparation

Slice the aubergine into thin rounds, spread the slices in a large tray and sprinkle with salt. Leave for 20 minutes to remove excess moisture. Pat dry with a paper towel and pass through the flour, shaking off any excess.

In a large frying pan, pour in enough olive oil to cover the base, and heat. Place the floured aubergine rounds into the oil and fry on each side until golden. Remove and drain on paper towel or greaseproof paper. Arrange carefully and keep to one side.

to prepare the cheese sauce

Melt the butter in a pan. Stir in the flour and cook gently to a paste. Add the warmed milk gradually, stirring all the time until smooth. Add the onion, bay leaf and nutmeg, and heat gently for 20 minutes to cook the flour. Pass through a strainer. Stir in the cheese and the cream. Remove from the heat and beat in the egg yolk. Season. Mix the prawns into the sauce. Arrange the aubergine slices on a baking sheet. Spoon over the cheese and prawn sauce. Sprinkle with the Parmesan and cook in a hot oven (400°F/200°C/Gas Mark 6) until golden-brown. Garnish with parsley and serve.

Cheese and Potato Croquettes

Croquetas de Patata y Queso

900 g/2 lb potatoes
2 egg yolks
55 g/2 oz butter
Salt and freshly ground
black pepper
Pinch of nutmeg
Dash of sherry
55 g/2 oz grated Parmesan
cheese
Pinch of dry mustard
2 Tbsp parsley, chopped
Seasoned flour
Egg wash (2 eggs beaten
with a little milk)
Breadcrumbs
Parsley, to garnish

preparation

Wash and peel the potatoes, and cut to an even size. Cook in salted water until soft; then drain. Put a lid on the pan of potatoes and place over a low heat to dry out, stirring occasionally to prevent burning.

Place the potatoes in a food processor with the yolks, butter and seasoning. Mix in the nutmeg, sherry, Parmesan cheese, mustard and parsley. The potatoes should be like a very firm mash. Overmixing will make them gluey, in which case some flour will have to be worked in by hand.

Check the mix is well seasoned and mould into cylinder shapes, measuring 13 by 5 cm/5 by 2 inches. Roll in seasoned flour, dip in egg wash and coat with breadcrumbs. Deep-fry in hot fat (365°F/185°C). When golden, drain well and serve garnished with parsley.

Note: If you want to keep the croquettes for cooking later, or the next day, place them carefully on a tray, cover with clingfilm and refrigerate.

Garlic Bread

Pan de Ajo

3 cloves garlic
225 g/8 oz butter, softened
to room temperature
1 Tbsp parsley, chopped
Salt and freshly ground
black pepper
1 large crusty loaf, or
6 small pitta breads

preparation

Peel the garlic by placing on a baking sheet in a hot oven (450°F/230°C/Gas Mark 8) for 10 minutes (the garlic will pop out of its skin). Crush the peeled garlic cloves in a garlic press, food processor or by the old-fashioned method of crushing under the blade of a large knife, with salt. Blend the crushed garlic into the butter. Add the chopped parsley and seasoning.

Place the bread in a hot oven (450°F/230°C/Gas Mark 8) for 15 minutes. If using pitta breads, sprinkle with a little water before placing in the oven to give a softer bread. Slice the loaf, smother with the butter and serve.

There are several savoury alternatives to this recipe:

Add 2 teaspoons of tomato purée to the butter, smother bread with the pink butter, and toast.

Use 170 g/6 oz butter and 57 g/2 oz grated cheese, in place of the 227 g/8 oz butter. Mix together with the flavourings. Heat the bread, slice, smother with the butter-cheese mix and place back in the oven to melt the cheese. Season and serve.

Garlic Mushrooms

Champiñones al Ajillo

85 g/3 oz butter
680 g/1½ lb mushrooms,
button or similar
A few drops of lemon juice
Salt and freshly ground
black pepper
3 tsp garlic, crushed
1 Tbsp coriander leaves or
parsley, chopped

preparation

Heat the butter in a large pan. Add the mushrooms and cook gently, covered, for 5 minutes, shaking occasionally.

Add the lemon juice and salt and pepper, and increase the heat, tossing the mushrooms well. Add the garlic, toss and cook for 2 minutes.

Add the coriander or parsley and cook for 1 minute. Remove from the heat and serve.

Stewed Giant Olives

Aceitunas Gigantes

1 jar large olives, cut around
the stone without
cutting through
1 medium onion, chopped
1 clove garlic, peeled and
part crushed
1 bay leaf
2 Tbsp olive oil
2 Tbsp red wine vinegar

preparation

This recipe makes 1½ pints of olives.

Put the ingredients in a pan. Cover with water, adding enough olive oil to put a slick on the top. Bring to the boil and simmer, covered, until soft, for 4 to 6 hours.

These will keep well in the refrigerator for 2 weeks.

Three Peppers in Tomato and Garlic

Pimientos en Tomate y Ajo

2 yellow peppers
2 red peppers
2 green peppers
170 ml/6 fl oz olive oil
1 Tbsp parsley, chopped
2 tsp garlic, crushed
225 g/8 oz fresh, preferably
small, or tinned
tomatoes
Salt and freshly ground
black pepper

preparation

Seed the peppers and cut into thin strips. Heat the oil in a large frying pan and cook the peppers gently for 2 to 3 minutes, stirring frequently. Add the parsley and garlic and cook for another couple of minutes.

Add the chopped tomatoes and their juice to the pan. Stir and season. Cover the pan and simmer gently for about 20 minutes, until the peppers are tender.

The sauce should be quite thick—if necessary, remove the peppers and boil rapidly to reduce the liquid. Check the seasoning.

This is a summer *tapa*, and may be eaten hot or cold; its flavour improves after one day.

Note: If you like spicy food, substitute chilli oil for the olive oil.

Cold Soup

Gazpacho

40 g/1½ oz soft white breadcrumbs
4 Tbsp olive oil
1 cucumber, chopped
1 green pepper, seeded
225 g/8 oz tin plum tomatoes
1 medium onion
1 tsp garlic, crushed
1 Tbsp lemon juice
Salt and freshly ground black pepper

preparation

Using a fork, mix the breadcrumbs and olive oil in a bowl to form a smooth paste.

Blend the remaining ingredients in a food processor, stir in the bread paste, season well and chill.

If you prefer a more liquid soup, add tomato juice and stir well.

Stuffed Peppers with Minced Chilli Beef

Pimientas Verdes con Picante

450 g/1 lb minced beef or pork
4 Tbsp oil (or 55 g/2 oz butter)
1 onion, finely chopped
2 tsp garlic, crushed
6 red chillies, finely chopped
½ tsp dried oregano
1 bay leaf
570 ml/1 pt water
Salt and freshly ground black pepper
2 tsp tomato purée
1 tsp basil, chopped
225 g/8 oz tin kidney beans
2 large tomatoes, peeled and chopped
3 large or 6 small green peppers
55 g/2 oz grated manchego cheese (see note, page 18)

to prepare the filling

Gently cook the meat in the oil or butter. Add the onion, garlic, chillies, oregano, bay leaf, water, salt, pepper, tomato purée and basil, and cook, stirring, until it comes to the boil. Lower heat and simmer for 45 minutes, stirring occasionally. Add the beans and tomato, season to taste and bring to the boil. Remove from heat.

to prepare the peppers

Remove the stalks. Plunge into boiling salted water and simmer for 5 minutes. Immediately cool in cold water and drain. For large peppers, cut in half lengthwise, and seed. Fill with meat mixture, sprinkle with cheese and bake at 400°F/200°C/Gas Mark 6 until the cheese melts. For small peppers, cut off the tops, and place aside. Carefully seed, core and trim the bases without making holes in them, so the peppers sit squarely. Fill with the meat and cheese. Place on a baking sheet with the top next to it and bake at 400°F/200°C/Gas Mark 6 until the cheese melts. Replace tops and serve.

Stuffed Tomatoes

Tomates Rellenos

8 small tomatoes, or 3 large
tomatoes
4 hard-boiled eggs, cooled
and peeled
6 Tbsp garlic mayonnaise
(see Smoked Fish
Mayonnaise and Garlic
Toast, page 21)
Salt and freshly ground
black pepper
1 Tbsp parsley, chopped
1 Tbsp white breadcrumbs,
if using large tomatoes

preparation

Skin the tomatoes, first by cutting out the core with a
sharp knife and making a '+' incision on the other end
of the tomato. Then place in a pan of boiling water
for 10 seconds, remove and plunge into a bowl of iced
or very cold water (this latter step is to stop the
tomatoes from cooking and going mushy).

Slice the tops off the tomatoes, and just enough of
their bases to remove the rounded ends so that they
will sit squarely on the plate. Keep the tops if using
small tomatoes, but discard those of large tomatoes.
Remove the seeds and insides, either with a teaspoon
or small, sharp knife.

Mash the eggs with the mayonnaise, salt, pepper and
parsley. Stuff the tomatoes, firmly pressing the filling
down. With small tomatoes, replace the lids at a
jaunty angle. If keeping to serve later, brush them
with olive oil and black pepper to prevent them from
drying out. Cover with clingfilm and keep.

For large tomatoes, the filling must be firm enough to
be sliced. If you make your own mayonnaise, thicken
it by using more egg yolks. If you use shop-bought
mayonnaise, add white breadcrumbs until the mixture
reaches the consistency of mashed potatoes. Season.
Fill the tomatoes, pressing down firmly until level.
Refrigerate for 1 hour, then slice with a sharp carving
knife into rings. Sprinkle with chopped parsley.

Tomato Salad with Olives

Ensalada de Tomate con Aceitunas

3 large tomatoes
½ medium red onion, finely sliced
A few black olives
Chives, to garnish

preparation

Slice the tomatoes horizontally. Arrange either in a large bowl with onion in between layers, or spread out on a large plate. Sprinkle with black olives.

For the vinaigrette
8 Tbsp olive oil
3 Tbsp red wine vinegar
½ tsp garlic, finely chopped
½ Tbsp sugar
Salt and freshly ground black pepper

to prepare the vinaigrette

Combine the olive oil, red wine vinegar, garlic and sugar in a bottle with a screw top. Shake hard until the dressing is emulsified. Add salt and pepper to taste, and shake again. Dredge the tomatoes with the dressing and serve garnished with chopped chives.

If keeping to serve later, add the vinaigrette 20 minutes before required. The vinaigrette will keep in the refrigerator for up to two weeks.

Artichoke Hearts with Tomato and Lemon

Alcachofas con Tomate y Limón

6 artichokes
Juice of 1 lemon
1 tsp flour
570 ml/1 pt cold water
Salt

For the sauce
85 g/3 oz butter
1 small onion, finely chopped
1 tsp garlic, crushed
4 rashers lean bacon or smoked ham, chopped
225 g/8 oz tin plum tomatoes or 2 large tomatoes, skinned, seeded and chopped
2 Tbsp parsley, chopped
Salt and freshly ground pepper
Juice of 2 lemons
The 6 cooked artichoke bottoms

preparation

Cut off the artichoke stalks and pull out the underneath leaves. With a large knife, cut through the artichoke, leaving only about 25 mm/1 inch at the bottom of the vegetable.

While holding the artichoke upside down, peel carefully with a small paring knife, removing all the leaf and any green part, and keeping the bottom as smooth as possible. If necessary, smooth with a peeler. Immediately rub with lemon and keep in lemon water.

Use a teaspoon or your thumb to remove the furry choke in the centre. It should come out easily. If you have problems, don't worry: it will come out easily after cooking, though it will be a little messy. Discard.

Mix the flour and water together, then add the salt and lemon juice. Pass through a strainer into a pan and bring to the boil, stirring constantly. Add the artichokes. Simmer gently until just tender, for about 20 minutes. Drain.

to prepare the sauce

Take the artichoke bottoms and cut into 5 or 6 triangles, by cutting each one in half, then each half into 2 or 3.

Melt the butter in a pan. Add the onion, garlic and bacon, and cook gently for 5 minutes.

Add the tomato and parsley. Season and bring to the boil. Pour in the lemon juice. Add the artichoke bottom pieces. Heat gently, stirring. If the mix is too tart, add a pinch of sugar.

Serve with crusty bread and a tomato salad.

Pickled Cucumber with Chillies

Conserva de Pepinillos con Picante

2 cucumbers
Salt
2 red chillies, or 1 Tbsp chilli oil
1 tsp garlic, crushed
Freshly ground black pepper
White wine vinegar
Sugar

preparation

Peel the cucumbers and slice finely. Spread on a tray and sprinkle with salt to remove the excess moisture. Leave for 2 hours.

Wash the salt off the cucumbers, and drain.

Chop the chillies, discarding the seeds. Mix the chillies with the cucumber and garlic, seasoning with freshly ground black pepper.

Place in a jar, preferably one with a screw-top. Cover with white wine vinegar and enough sugar to remove the acidity. Stir well and cover.

This may be eaten the next day—or even a year hence.

Mint and Chilli Cucumber

Pepinillos con Picante y Menta

1 cucumber
1 large tomato
½ tsp garlic, chopped
Bunch of mint, chopped
Small pot of plain yoghurt
Small pot of soured cream
1 tsp ground cumin
2 red chillies, seeded and chopped
Salt and freshly ground black pepper

preparation

Shred the cucumber, sprinkle with salt and put aside in a strainer while you prepare the other ingredients.

Peel the tomato by placing in boiling water for 10 seconds and then plunging into iced or very cold water to loosen the skin. Chop into little squares and discard the seeds.

Wash the excess moisture off the cucumber and drain well, squeezing out any moisture.

Mix all the ingredients together in a bowl, season well and chill before serving.

Green Beans Tapa

Tapa de Judías Verdes

450 g/1 lb French beans,
trimmed
55 g/2 oz butter
4 Tbsp olive oil
½ medium onion, finely
chopped
Salt and freshly ground
black pepper
285 ml/½ pt chicken stock
1 Tbsp garlic, crushed

preparation

Place the beans in a pan of boiling salted water and cook for 6 to 8 minutes, until the beans are no longer raw but remain fairly firm. Drain well.

Melt the butter in a pan, add the olive oil, and heat. Add the onion and cook gently for 3 to 4 minutes. Add the beans, salt and pepper, and toss together. Add the chicken stock and the garlic. Cover and cook until tender, approximately 10 minutes. Season well and serve.

Stuffed Courgettes

<u>C a l a b a c í n   E s t o f a d o</u>

6 small courgettes
½ medium onion, finely
chopped
1 Tbsp olive oil
225 g/½ lb lamb, minced
3 rashers lean bacon,
finely chopped
Salt and freshly ground
black pepper
1 tsp tomato purée
½ tsp sugar
1 tsp garlic, crushed
1 Tbsp water
1 tomato, peeled and
chopped
½ small pot plain yoghurt
12 mint leaves, chopped
30 g/1 oz grated Parmesan
cheese
Extra chopped mint,
to garnish

preparation

Trim off the ends of the courgettes and discard. Place
the courgettes in boiling salted water for 5 minutes.
Cut in half lengthwise and, with a teaspoon, scoop
out the seeds along the centre.

Gently cook the onion in the oil until soft. Add the
lamb, bacon, salt and pepper. Stir. Add the tomato
purée, sugar, garlic and water. Cook until the meat is
cooked through, for about 15 minutes.

Stir in the tomato, yoghurt and mint leaves. Spoon
this mix into the hollowed-out courgettes.

Sprinkle with the Parmesan cheese and black pepper.
Bake in a hot oven (400°F/200°C/Gas Mark 6) until
the cheese melts. Sprinkle with the remaining mint
leaves and serve.

Courgettes with Dill

Calabacines a las Hierbas

4 Tbsp olive oil
30 g/1 oz butter
1 onion, chopped
1 tsp garlic, crushed
450 g/1 lb courgettes,
topped, tailed and sliced
in thick rounds
½ tsp freshly ground black
pepper
2 tsp paprika
1 Tbsp dill, chopped (not the
stalks)
Salt, to taste

preparation

Heat oil and butter in a large frying pan. Gently cook the onion and garlic until soft. Turn up the heat, add the courgettes and black pepper, and toss.

Cook for 5 to 10 minutes, turning the courgette slices to cook both sides.

When the courgette slices are browning, add the paprika and dill. Season and serve.

Roast Potatoes in Sweet Hot Sauce

Patatas Bravas

1 onion, chopped
2 Tbsp olive oil
1 bay leaf
2 red chillies
2 tsp garlic, crushed
1 Tbsp tomato purée
½ Tbsp sugar (up to 1 Tbsp,
if the sauce is too tart
for your liking)
1 Tbsp soy sauce
450 g/1 lb tin plum
tomatoes, chopped
150 g/5 fl oz white wine
Salt and freshly ground
black pepper
8 medium potatoes

to prepare the sauce

Gently cook the onions in the oil with the bay leaf. When soft, add the chillies, garlic, tomato purée, sugar and soy sauce. Cook for a further 5 minutes on a low heat.

Add the chopped tomatoes and white wine. Stir and bring to the boil. Simmer for 10 minutes. Season to taste. This sauce should be slightly sweet; the flavour of the tomatoes should not dominate it.

to prepare the potatoes

Cut the potatoes like small roast potatoes.

Grease a baking sheet. Season the potatoes well and brush with melted butter. Roast in a hot oven (450°F/230°C/Gas Mark 8) until golden.

Pour the tomato sauce over the potatoes and serve.

Garlic Potatoes

Patatas al Alioli

8 medium potatoes
2 egg yolks
1 tsp garlic, crushed
2 tsp vinegar
⅛ tsp dry mustard
Salt and freshly ground
black pepper
340 ml/12 fl oz olive oil
Approximately 2 tsp boiling
water

preparation

Prepare the potatoes as for Roast Potatoes in Sweet Hot Sauce (see above).

Place yolks, garlic, vinegar, mustard and seasoning in a bowl or food processor. Gradually pour on the oil, very slowly, whisking or whizzing continually. Add the boiling water, whisking well. Pour the dressing over the potatoes, stir to mix, and serve.

Refried Kidney Beans

Habitas Refritas

450 g/1 lb tin kidney beans
1 red chilli, seeded and chopped
1 medium onion, finely chopped
2 tsp garlic, crushed
1 tsp paprika
Salt and freshly ground black pepper
1 1/2 pts water
6 rashers lean bacon, rind removed
55 g/2 oz butter
Parsley, to serve

preparation

Place first 7 ingredients in a pan, bring to the boil, and simmer for 40 minutes.

Place one-quarter of the total in a food processor and purée. Remix the puréed beans with the whole beans.

Chop the bacon and place in boiling water for 10 minutes to remove the saltiness. Remove from the water, and drain.

Heat the butter in a frying pan and fry the bacon. Add the beans, little by little, and mash with the back of a spoon. Season well.

The beans should go into a thick purée. Season, sprinkle with parsley and serve. The more often you refry the beans, the better they taste.

Stuffed Cabbage Leaves

Repollo Estofado

1 large green cabbage, or
cos lettuce, or 1 lb/450 g
spinach
1 tsp paprika
Salt and freshly ground
black pepper
½ Tbsp parsley, chopped
450 g/1 lb lamb, minced
55 g/2 oz butter
1 onion, finely chopped
1 tsp garlic, crushed
1 red chilli, seeded
and chopped
1 tsp tomato purée
230 ml/8 fl oz tomato juice
1 tsp soy sauce
285 ml/½ pt chicken stock
85 g/3 oz mushrooms,
finely chopped
170 g/6 oz salted peanuts,
crushed

preparation

Remove the dirty outer leaves from the cabbage.
Carefully pick off the large whole leaves and cut out
the thick part of the stalk. Put the leaves in a pan of
boiling salted water to soften. Simmer for 5 minutes.

Remove the leaves and plunge into cold water. When
cold, carefully lay out the leaves on a clean tea towel
or paper towel, and pat dry with another tea towel
placed on top. Arrange with the inside of the leaves
facing towards you.

to prepare the filling

In a large bowl work the paprika, salt, pepper and
parsley into the minced lamb.

Melt the butter in a pan. Add the onion and cook
gently until softened. Add the lamb, garlic, chilli and
tomato purée. Pour in the tomato juice, soy sauce and
stock, and stir. Add the mushrooms and peanuts.

Simmer for 30 minutes, stirring occasionally. Remove
from the heat and cool. Check the seasoning. If the
mixture is still runny, add a small amount of flour.

When cold, spoon small amounts of the mixture into
the centre of the cabbage leaves, folding the outside
edges over and placing the folded side, base down, in
an oiled roasting tin.

Note: If your leaves are a little ragged or small, use
two leaves to wrap around the lamb mixture.

When all the cabbage parcels are in the roasting tin,
pour in enough chicken stock to half-cover them.
Cover the tray with foil. Pierce with a fork to allow
the steam to escape and poach in the oven for 20
minutes, at 400°F/200°C/Gas Mark 6.

Remove carefully with a large spoon and moisten
with a little of the poaching liquor.

opposite: **Stuffed Cabbage Leaves**

Corn on the Cob with Garlic Butter

Mazorca con
Mantequilla de Ajo

4 fresh corn on the cob
Garlic butter (see recipe for
Garlic Bread, page 40)
Salt and freshly ground
black pepper

preparation

Remove the outer green leaves from the fresh corn.
Place in boiling salted water with a drop of olive oil.
Simmer for 20 minutes, or until the corn is cooked
and tender.

Remove from the heat and drain. Smother liberally
with garlic butter, season well and serve.

Egg & Cheese

Goat's Cheese with Tarragon and Garlic Marinade

Queso de Cabra con Ajo y Estragón

Goat's cheese

For the marinade
Generous 1 l/1¾ pts olive oil
1 Tbsp white wine vinegar
1 bunch of tarragon, with crushed stalks
1 bulb of garlic
Black peppercorns

preparation

Try to get genuine manchego cheese (see note, page 18) for this recipe. If this is not possible, use a mild, milky flavoured goat's cheese.

Leaving the rind on the cheese, chop it into even bite-sized chunks.

Mix together the ingredients for the marinade. Cover and refrigerate the cheese, and leave for at least 4 days in a jar or porcelain pot before eating.

Chilli with Manchego Cheese

Quejo Manchego con Salsa Picante

6 red chillies, seeded and chopped
240 ml/8 fl oz olive oil
Salt and freshly ground black pepper
225 g/8 oz manchego cheese (see note, page 18)
Lime wedges, to serve

preparation

Blend the chillies with the olive oil, adding a good pinch each of salt and pepper.

Cut the cheese into small, spikable cubes.

Pour the oil over the cheese and marinate for at least 2 hours. Serve with lime wedges.

Spanish Omelette

Tortilla Española

Basic recipe for 1 omelette
3 potatoes (or an equal amount of potato to onion)
3 Tbsp olive oil
1 onion, finely chopped or sliced
Salt and freshly ground black pepper
3 eggs
Chives, to garnish

preparation

Note: When frying, if the mixture becomes a little too dry, add more oil.

Wash the potatoes. (It is optional to peel them— Spaniards will never put unpeeled potato in an omelette, but other people like to.) Slice very finely and place in a pan of cold salted water. Bring to the boil and cook for 5 minutes (parboil). If preferred, the potatoes for this dish can be sautéed.

Place a frying pan on the heat and heat the oil. Add the onion carefully, as the oil might spit. Stir while cooking. Add the potato slices. Shake the pan, and stir to prevent any sticking to the bottom. Season lightly with salt and pepper.

In a bowl, beat the eggs and season well.

Lower the heat slightly under the potatoes and onion, and cook, tossing until golden-brown. Add the potato and onion to the egg mix, and stir well. Replace the pan on the heat and when hot pour the mixture into it. It will seal immediately. Cook for 2 minutes, then turn the omelette by one of 2 methods: either slip the omelette into another hot pan brushed with oil by placing pan no. 2 over pan no. 1 and flip it; or place a large plate over the omelette, flip the omelette onto the plate and slide it back into the pan so the uncooked side is now over the heat. Cook for 1 minute.

Leave to cool, garnish with chopped chives and slice to serve. The omelette should be thick, firm and cake-like, quite unlike the French omelette.

Note: Many ingredients and flavourings may be used (or used up!) in omelettes, for instance green peppers (sliced and added to the onions), mushrooms, cooked ham, cheese, and so on.

opposite: **Spanish Omelette**

Egg and Garlic Fried Bread

Pan Frito con Ajo y Huevo

3 eggs
A few drops of warm water
2 tsp garlic, crushed
Salt and freshly ground
black pepper
3 Tbsp olive oil
6 slices of bread

preparation

Beat the eggs in a bowl with a few drops of warm water. Add the crushed garlic and seasoning to the egg and mix well.

Heat the oil in a frying pan. Dip the bread in the egg so that both sides are covered, and place in the pan. Fry until each side is golden brown.

Note: The oil must be hot for this recipe to seal the egg immediately (watch for a wavy look on the pan bottom). Also, the bread must be turned quickly to prevent the garlic from burning.

Paella Croquettes

Croquetas de Paella

Generous 450 g/1 lb risotto
rice
1 medium onion, roughly
chopped
1 bay leaf
1 tsp garlic, crushed
1 chicken stock cube
1 Tbsp olive oil
2 tsp turmeric
2 times the quantity of
water to rice (ideally, use
good chicken stock)
280 g/10 oz chorizo sausage
and smoked ham, mixed,
preferably in equal
quantities (any spiced
salamis or cooked meats
may be used for this
recipe)
Seasoned flour
Egg wash (2 eggs, beaten
with a little milk)
Breadcrumbs
Oil, to fry
Parsley, to serve

preparation

Put the rice in a pan, and add the onion, bay leaf, garlic, stock cube, olive oil and turmeric. Pour the hot water over the mix.

Put on the heat and bring the mix to the boil. Turn down the heat and simmer until the rice is soft and has absorbed all the water (approximately 15 minutes). Remove from the heat and leave to cool.

Mince the meat in a food processor and add to the cold rice, mixing in well. There should be an equal ratio of rice to meat in the balls. The mixture should be slightly moist but easy to form into small balls. If your mix is too wet, add a little flour or breadcrumbs to it.

Form the mix into even size balls. Roll them in the flour until lightly covered.

Roll in the egg wash and then in the breadcrumbs. At this stage the croquettes may be refrigerated and kept until the next day.

Deep-fry in hot oil (365°F/185°C), until golden and crispy on the outside. Sprinkle with parsley and serve.

Note: The croquettes may be reheated in a microwave.

Aves

Tapas

Chicken

Chicken in Batter with Honey and Mustard

Pollo Rebozado con Miel y Mostaza

3 chicken breasts, cut into 25 mm/1 in cubes
Salt and freshly ground black pepper
2 eggs
Flour, to coat
4 Tbsp olive oil
8 Tbsp runny honey
1 tsp French mustard
1 tsp soy sauce

preparation

Place the chicken pieces in a bowl. Season. Break the eggs over the chicken pieces and mix in thoroughly, using your hands.

Add enough flour to make a thick coating over the chicken. The egg and flour mixture should be of a consistency where it stops just short of dripping.

Heat the oil in a frying pan and fry the chicken until golden, turning frequently, for about 15 minutes.

Remove from the heat; sprinkle with salt and pepper.

Blend the honey with the mustard and soy sauce. Drizzle the honey mixture over the chicken and serve immediately.

Spanish Chicken Pie

E m p a n a d a   d e   P o l l o

1 lb pastry and topping, as
for recipe for Spanish
Squid Pie (see
page 24)

For the filling
4 Tbsp olive oil
1 onion, chopped
225 g/½ lb bacon, chopped
3 tsp garlic, crushed
1 green pepper, seeded
and sliced
2 chillies, seeded and
chopped
1 tsp paprika
125 g/4½ oz button
mushrooms, sliced
100 g/3½ oz raisins
(optional)
2 tsp parsley, chopped
2 tsp soy sauce
155 ml/5 fl oz dry white
wine
285 ml/½ pt chicken stock
30 g/1 oz butter
900 g/2 lb chicken meat,
boned and cubed

preparation

Heat the oil. Gently cook the onion and bacon in it.

Add the garlic, pepper, chillies, paprika, sliced mushrooms and raisins, if using. Stir and add the parsley and soy sauce. Pour on the wine and stock, stir and simmer for 20 minutes.

In a separate pan, melt the butter and add the chicken. Toss until browned all over and add to the vegetables. Stir and simmer for 5 minutes.

Remove from heat.

Grease and line a paella dish (dish for 2) with half the dough. Add the filling; the pie will rise to fill the dish. Cover with slices of tomato and a little salt.

Roll out the remaining dough, sealing the edges well. Glaze with the egg yolk and decorate as desired. Leave to stand for 10 minutes before baking.

Bake in the oven at 400°F/200°C/Gas Mark 6 for 30 minutes. Leave to cool, and slice to serve.

Note: If you wish to make individual *empanadas*, cut out 15 cm/6 inch rounds of pastry. Place the filling in one half and cover with the remaining dough, sealing the edges well.

Chicken Livers with Sherry Vinegar

Higaditos de Pollo con Vinagre de Jerez

454 g/1 lb chicken livers
1 tsp paprika
1 tsp garlic, crushed
½ tsp each salt and freshly ground black pepper
55 g/2 oz butter, melted
½ onion, finely chopped
4 Tbsp sherry vinegar
1 tsp sugar
285 ml/½ pt chicken stock
55 g/2 oz butter

preparation

Wash and trim the chicken livers to remove the green bile sacs and any gristle.

Mix the paprika, garlic, salt and pepper together in a bowl. Toss the livers to cover in the mix.

Heat the 57 g/2 oz of melted butter in a large frying pan. Cook the livers over high heat in the butter, stirring continuously, until sealed and browned all over. Place livers in a warmed bowl.

Add the onion to the pan and soften over a lower heat. Turn up the heat again, add the vinegar and sugar, and cook until the vinegar is almost dry. Add the stock, stir, and reduce to half the quantity.

Take the remaining 57 g/2 oz butter, break into small pieces and stir until it melts into the liquid. Check the seasoning and pour the sauce over the livers. Serve in a large bowl or in smaller, individual ones.

Chicken in Garlic Sauce

<u>P o l l o   a l   A j i l l o</u>

900 g/2 lb chicken wings, or
3 chicken breasts
Enough seasoned flour to
coat the chicken pieces
4 Tbsp olive oil
2 Tbsp butter
5½ Tbsp white wine
4 Tbsp of chicken stock
3 tsp garlic, crushed
1 Tbsp parsley, chopped
Generous Tbsp sherry
Generous Tbsp brandy
Salt and freshly ground
black pepper
Parsley, to garnish

preparation

Cut the chicken into small chunks and toss in the flour until evenly coated.

Heat the oil and butter in a pan. Cook the chicken in the pan until golden, turning quickly to seal all sides.

Add the wine, chicken stock, garlic and parsley. Simmer to reduce the liquid by half. Stir. Add the sherry and brandy.

Season and serve garnished with the parsley.

Chicken and Bacon with Mussels

Pollo con Bacon y Mejillones

4 Tbsp olive oil
1 onion, chopped
6 rashers of bacon, cut into strips
3 chicken breasts, cubed and tossed in seasoned flour
155 ml/5 fl oz dry white wine
340 g/12 oz mushrooms, finely sliced
2 tsp garlic, crushed
570 ml/1 pt fish or chicken stock
900 g/2 lb mussels, cleaned (see tip, page 23)
Salt and freshly ground black pepper
2 Tbsp parsley, chopped

preparation

Heat the oil in a pan. Add the onion and cook gently.

Turn up the heat, add the bacon and stir. Add the chicken pieces and stir again to seal the meat all over.

In a separate pan, heat the wine, mushrooms and garlic until reduced by half, then add to the chicken.

Add the chicken or fish stock and bring to the boil.

Add the mussels. Cover the pan with a lid, and shake. Cook until the mussels open. Season well, spoon into hot bowls and garnish with the parsley.

Meat Tapas

Carnes

Lamb with Apricot Sauce

Cordero con Salsa de Albaricoque

680 g/1½ lb lamb fillet
Salt and freshly ground
black pepper
Oil or butter, to fry

For the sauce
4 Tbsp vegetable oil
55 g/2 oz butter
1 tsp garlic, crushed
170 g/6 oz tin apricots,
puréed
70 g/2½ oz peanut butter
Juice of 1 lemon, to taste
Salt and freshly ground
black pepper
Parsley, to garnish

preparation

Cut the lamb into 25 mm/1 inch cubes and season.
Thread onto skewers and grill, or fry in hot oil or melted
butter in a pan until tender, approximately 5 minutes.

to prepare the sauce

Melt the oil and butter together and add the garlic.
Whisk in the puréed apricots and the peanut butter.

Do not allow the peanut butter to become too hot;
remove from the pan when half-melted.

Add the lemon juice and season to taste. Serve with
the lamb pieces. Garnish with parsley.

Marinated Lamb Cutlets

Chuletas de Cordero Marinadas

6 lamb cutlets, trimmed of excess fat

For the marinade
2 tsp paprika
1 tsp ground cumin
1 tsp turmeric
1 red chilli, chopped
1 Tbsp mint, chopped
4 Tbsp olive oil

preparation

Combine all the marinade ingredients and brush liberally over the cutlets.

Marinate in the refrigerator for at least 1 hour.

To cook, bake at 400°F/200°C/Gas Mark 6 until cooked through (approximately 20 to 25 minutes), or grill, allowing 6 minutes each side. Although these cutlets don't really need a sauce, the following soured cream-based dip complements them well:

236 ml/8 fl oz soured cream
57 g/2 oz dried apricots, finely chopped
Freshly ground black pepper

Combine the three ingredients in a bowl or food processor and serve on the side.

Meatballs with Garlic and Tomato

Albondigas con Ajo y Tomate

900 g/2 lb lamb, minced
15 g/½ oz breadcrumbs
Salt and freshly ground
black pepper
2 tsp garlic, crushed
½ tsp ground nutmeg
2 eggs
1 heaped Tbsp seasoned
flour
4 Tbsp olive oil
1 large onion, chopped
1 green pepper, cut into
strips
225 g/8 oz tin chopped plum
tomatoes, or two large
tomatoes, skinned and
roughly chopped
1 Tbsp tomato purée
155 ml/5 fl oz dry red wine
170 ml/6 fl oz chicken stock
1 Tbsp parsley, chopped

preparation

In a large bowl, mix the lamb with the breadcrumbs
and season well. Add 1 teaspoon of the crushed garlic,
the nutmeg and the eggs. Form into small meatballs,
then roll in the flour.

Heat the oil in a large pan, and cook the onion and
green pepper until tender. Add the meatballs and fry
until browned on all sides, stirring well. Add the
remaining garlic, tomatoes, tomato purée, wine and
stock. Cover and simmer for 40 minutes.

Season, stir in the parsley and serve. Add a little sugar
if the sauce is too sharp.

Note: These may be prepared in advance and
then reheated.

Spanish Smoked Ham

Jamón Serrano

340 g/³/₄ lb jamón serrano,
Smithfield country-cured
ham, prosciutto *or*
Westphalian ham, finely
sliced and rolled
680 g/1¹/₂ lb stuffed olives
Lemon wedges, to serve

preparation

Jamón serrano is a smoked ham from Spain. It is usually served thinly sliced and is delicious with melon.

Spike cocktail sticks with a roll of ham and an olive, alternately, and serve with lemon wedges.

Spanish Smoked Ham with Tomato and Garlic Toast

Pan con Tomate y Ajo y Jamón Serrano

6 slices of garlic bread (see
Garlic Bread, page 40)
2 large tomatoes, sliced and
dredged with vinaigrette
(see page 45)
227 g/½ lb jamón serrano,
Smithfield country-cured
ham, prosciutto or
Westphalian ham,
finely sliced
1 red onion, finely sliced
140 g/5 oz stuffed olives,
chopped

preparation

Prepare the garlic bread and bake in a hot oven until crisp around the edges.

Place a slice of tomato and a slice of ham on the toast, and top with the onion and olives.

This makes an ideal savoury finger-food.

Baked Chorizo Sausage

Chorizos Horneados

preparation

This delicious spicy sausage is readily available in a number of delicatessens.

Slice the sausage into rounds, place in a hot oven (480°F/240°C/Gas Mark 9) and bake until just beginning to crisp around the edges, approximately 10 minutes. Serve with plenty of bread.

Chunked Pork in Orange Sauce

C e r d o   a   l a   N a r a n j a

55 g/2 oz butter or 4 Tbsp olive oil
1 small onion, finely sliced
680 g/1½ lb pork fillet, cut into 25 mm/1 in cubes
Grated peel of 2 oranges
Juice of 3 oranges
170 ml/6 fl oz chicken stock
2 green chillies, chopped, or 2 tsp chilli paste
1 tsp garlic, crushed
1 Tbsp coriander or parsley, chopped
2 tsp cornflour
1 Tbsp cold water
Salt and freshly ground black pepper
Parsley, to garnish

preparation

In a large frying pan, heat the butter or oil. Sauté the onion until soft and golden, and place aside.

Add the pork to the pan and cook, turning until it is browned on all sides.

Combine the orange peel, orange juice, stock, chilli, garlic and coriander or parsley together, and pour over the pork. Bring to the boil and add the onion slices. Simmer for 10 minutes. Place in a warm bowl.

Mix the cornflour and water and add to the sauce to thicken it. Stir, season and pour over the meat. Garnish with parsley and serve.

Meat and Vegetable Soup

Caldo Gallego

55 g/2 oz butter
1 onion, chopped
450 g/1 lb bacon or ham
½ tsp garlic, crushed
2 1/4 pts stock or water
680 g/1½ lb potatoes,
peeled and cut into
small chunks
1 small, firm green cabbage,
finely chopped
Freshly ground black pepper
Crusty bread, to serve

preparation

Note: If using pork knuckle, simmer for 1½ hours first.

Melt the butter in a large saucepan. Add the onion and cook gently until soft. Stir in the bacon and garlic.

Pour the stock or water over the garlic and onion, add the potatoes, cover and cook for 15 minutes. Add the cabbage and cook for a further 5 minutes.

Remove lid, and sprinkle with black pepper. The soup should be thick; if you need to thicken, remove half the greens and potato and mash before returning to the pan.

Season and serve in bowls, with crusty bread.

Kidneys in Sherry Sauce

Riñones en Salsa de Jerez

680 g/1½ lb lamb or veal
kidneys
170 ml/6 fl oz olive oil
2 tsp garlic, crushed
1 tsp paprika
2 onions, chopped
8 Tbsp sherry
284 ml/½ pt chicken stock
Salt and freshly ground
black pepper
4 tsp parsley, chopped
3 slices of bread

preparation

Clean the kidneys, removing the hard core and any fat. Slice thinly with a sharp knife.

Bring a pan of water to the boil and plunge the kidneys in for one minute to remove the bitterness.

Heat the oil and fry half the kidneys, with 1 teaspoon of the garlic and ½ teaspoon of the paprika. Cook quickly, stirring so that the garlic does not burn. When cooked, blend in a food processor. Keep to one side.

In the same pan, cook the onions until soft. Place the remaining kidneys in the pan with the other teaspoon of the garlic and ½ teaspoon of paprika, and the sherry and stock. Bring to the boil.

Lower the heat, add the puréed kidneys, stir and simmer until the whole kidneys are tender (approximately 5 minutes). Season and serve garnished with chopped parsley, and bread.

Fried Lamb with Lemon Juice

Cordero Frito con Limón

800 g/1¾ lb trimmed tender
lamb, in strips
Salt and freshly ground
black pepper
2 Tbsp olive oil
1 onion, chopped
2 cloves garlic, finely
chopped
2 tsp paprika
230 ml/8 fl oz stock or water
Juice of 1 lemon
2 Tbsp parsley, finely
chopped

preparation

Season the lamb with salt and pepper. Heat the oil in a heatproof casserole over a very high heat and add the meat in handfuls. Add the onion and a little garlic, and keep turning the meat with a wooden spoon. Add more meat and garlic as each batch seals, with more oil if necessary.

When the meat is golden and the onion is soft, sprinkle with paprika and add the stock or water. Continue cooking over a medium heat until the liquid is almost dry.

Sprinkle with the lemon juice and parsley, cover and simmer for 5 minutes. Season to taste and serve.

Small Spicy Moorish Kebabs

Pinchitos Morunos

2 cloves garlic, finely
chopped
2 tsp salt
1 tsp mild curry powder
½ tsp coriander seeds
1 tsp paprika
¼ tsp dried thyme
Freshly ground black pepper
3 Tbsp olive oil
1 Tbsp lemon juice
Lime wedges, to serve
450 g/1 lb lean pork, cut
into small cubes

preparation

Crush the chopped garlic with the salt using a pestle and mortar (or the flat of a knife on a board).

Work the curry powder, coriander seeds, paprika, thyme, pepper, olive oil and lemon juice into the garlic and salt. Set the marinade aside in a shallow dish.

Remove any excess fat from the pork and chop into small bite-sized cubes. Skewer the meat, 3 to 4 cubes to a small stick, and turn the kebabs in the shallow dish to coat thoroughly with the marinade. Leave to marinate for at least a couple of hours. The longer you leave them, the better the flavour.

Arrange the kebabs, spreading them well apart, on foil under the grill, or on a barbecue. Cook under (or over) a high heat until the meat is browned on the outside and cooked through. This should take about 3 minutes on each side.

Serve immediately with lime wedges.

Note: Europe's first kebabs were brought by the Arabs from North Africa. They are eaten everywhere in Spain as a *tapa*, though nowadays they are made from pork, rather than the original lamb. Spices for them are sold ready-mixed in southern Spain. The curry powder used in this recipe contains cumin and other herbs identical to those used in Spain.